EASY APPETIZER COOKBOOK

50 APPETIZER RECIPES FOR ANY OCCASION

By
Chef Maggie Chow
Copyright © 2015 by Saxonberg Associates
All rights reserved

Published by
BookSumo, a division of Saxonberg Associates
http://www.booksumo.com/

INTRODUCTION

Welcome to *The Effortless Chef Series*! Thank you for taking the time to download the *Easy Appetizer Cookbook*. Come take a journey with me into the delights of easy cooking. The point of this cookbook and all my cookbooks is to exemplify the effortless nature of cooking simply.

In this book we focus on Appetizers. You will find that even though the recipes are simple, the taste of the dishes is quite amazing.

So will you join me in an adventure of simple cooking? If the answer is yes (and I hope it is) please consult the table of contents to find the dishes you are most interested in. Once you are ready jump right in and start cooking.

— Chef Maggie Chow

Table of Contents

Introduction 2

Table of Contents 3

Any Issues? Contact Me 9

Legal Notes 10

Common Abbreviations 11

Chapter 1: Easy Appetizer Recipes 12

    Honey Horseradish Steak 12

    Southeast Asian Spring Rolls 15

    Healthy Veggie Bites 18

    Tangy Cheese Appetizer 20

    Mediterranean Appetizer 22

    Upstate Maine Appetizer 25

Mexican Style Festive Cheesecakes 27

Gouda and Shrimp Cake 30

Mozzarella, Tomatoes, and Basil Appetizer 33

Summer Soiree Shrimp 35

Jalapeno Jelly Sausage 37

Pepper Tomatoes and Eggplant 39

Bacon and Chestnuts 41

Bread for Celebrations 43

2 Cheese Spinach Bake 45

Zucchini and Romano Roast 47

Scallops for the Banquet 49

Sweet Beef Cocktails 51

Apricot and Brie Puff Pastry 54

Mexican Appetizer 56

Easy Devils on Horseback 58

Spicy Cheese Appetizer 60

Chinese Dumplings 62

Spicy Chicken Wings ... 64

Festive Bruschetta Appetizer ... 66

Springtime Party Shrimp ... 68

Cute Little Sweet Sausages ... 70

Rustic Cheddar and Onion Baguette ... 72

Parmesan Rolls ... 74

Apples and Beef ... 76

Bacon Wrapper ... 78

Caprese Sandwiches ... 80

Festive Sandwich ... 82

Countryside Sausage Appetizer ... 84

Chinese Party Wontons ... 86

Creamy Salmon and Tomatoes ... 88

Appetizers for March ... 90

Crescents and Cheese ... 92

Basil Zucchini Bites ... 94

Sweet Peas ... 96

New York Style Pizza Bites 98
Little Japanese Meatballs 100
Pimentos and Blue Cheese 102
Authentic Guacamole 104
Jalapeno Bites 106
Toasted Party Pecans 108
Red and Green Salad 110
Mediterranean Pitas 112
Catalina's Cuban Sandwich 114
Deviled Eggs Japanese Style 116
(デビルド卵) 116
Rosemary Olive Tapas 119
Nutty Brie and Bread 121
Barcelona Style Almonds 123
Spicy Sherry Mushrooms 125
(Champinones Al Ajillo) 125
Garlic Potatoes 127

Classical Spanish Tomato Tapas 129

Sausage Empanada 131

Fish and Chips in Spain 134

Classic Dijon Potato Tapas 137

Prawn Tapas Spanish Style 139

Flame Broiled Chicken 141

Traditional Tomato Tapas 143

(Tomates Rellenos) 143

Sevilla 145

Real Spanish Tapas 147

Cilantro Shrimp Tapas 150

Honey Mustard Chicken Breast Girona Style Tapas 152

Yummiest Potato Tapas 154

Fennel and Coriander Olives 157

Orange Blossom Bread Sticks 159

THANKS FOR READING! NOW LET'S TRY SOME **SUSHI** AND **DUMP DINNERS**.. 161

Easy Appetizer Cookbook   7

Come On.. 163

Let's Be Friends :)... 163

Can I Ask A Favour?.. 164

Interested in Other Easy Cookbooks? 165

ANY ISSUES? CONTACT ME

If you find that something important to you is missing from this book please contact me at maggie@booksumo.com.

I will try my best to re-publish a revised copy taking your feedback into consideration and let you know when the book has been revised with you in mind.

:)

— Chef Maggie Chow

Legal Notes

ALL RIGHTS RESERVED. NO PART OF THIS BOOK MAY BE REPRODUCED OR TRANSMITTED IN ANY FORM OR BY ANY MEANS. PHOTOCOPYING, POSTING ONLINE, AND / OR DIGITAL COPYING IS STRICTLY PROHIBITED UNLESS WRITTEN PERMISSION IS GRANTED BY THE BOOK'S PUBLISHING COMPANY. LIMITED USE OF THE BOOK'S TEXT IS PERMITTED FOR USE IN REVIEWS WRITTEN FOR THE PUBLIC AND/OR PUBLIC DOMAIN.

COMMON ABBREVIATIONS

cup(s)	C.
tablespoon	tbsp
teaspoon	tsp
ounce	oz.
pound	lb

*All units used are standard American measurements

Chapter 1: Easy Appetizer Recipes

Honey Horseradish Steak

Ingredients

- 1 (1/2 lb) trimmed beef skirt steak, flattened with a mallet
- 2 tsps salt, divided
- 1 tsp ground black pepper, divided
- 2 tbsps honey, or to taste - divided
- 2 tbsps prepared horseradish
- 2 tbsps mayonnaise
- 1/2 tsp Worcestershire sauce

Directions

- Place your steak on a piece of parchment paper that is double the size of the steak.
- Coat one side of the steak with half a tsp pepper, 1 tsp salt, and 1 tbsps honey.
- Fold the paper over the steak and flip everything.
- Now coat the other side with the same amount of each ingredient.

- Wrap the steak completely in the paper and place everything in a plastic sealable bag.
- Put the steak in the fridge overnight.
- Get your grill hot and coat the grate with oil.
- Grill the steak for 60 secs then flip and cook it for 60 more secs.
- Continue flipping and grilling the steak every 60 secs 6 more times.
- Place the steak on some foil and wrap it.
- Leave the meat to sit for 7 mins then julienne the steak.
- Get a bowl, combine: Worcestershire, horseradish, and mayo.
- Use the topping or dip for your steak when serving it.
- Enjoy.

Amount per serving (5 total)

Timing Information:

Preparation	15 m
Cooking	5 m
Total Time	8 h 25 m

Nutritional Information:

Calories	110 kcal
Fat	6.3 g
Carbohydrates	8.2g
Protein	5.6 g
Cholesterol	12 mg
Sodium	997 mg

* Percent Daily Values are based on a 2,000 calorie diet.

Southeast Asian Spring Rolls

Ingredients

- 1 tbsp vegetable oil
- 1 lb ground beef
- 2 cloves garlic, crushed
- 1/2 C. chopped onion
- 1/2 C. minced carrots
- 1/2 C. chopped green onions
- 1/2 C. thinly sliced green cabbage
- 1 tsp ground black pepper
- 1 tsp salt
- 1 tsp garlic powder
- 1 tsp soy sauce
- 30 wonton wrappers
- 2 C. vegetable oil for frying

Directions

- Stir fry your beef until it is fully done then place the meat to the side and remove the excess drippings but leave about a tbsp.
- Begin to stir fry your onion and garlic in the drippings for 3 mins then add in the cabbage, beef, green onions, and carrots.

- Stir the mix then add in the soy sauce, pepper, garlic powder, and salt.
- Stir the mix again to work in the spices then shut the heat and let the mix cool.
- Lay out some wrappers and layer 3 tbsps of the mix in the middle of each.
- Shape the wrappers into dumplings then crimp and seal the edges with a bit of water.
- Get half an inch of oil hot in a pan then begin to fry your dumplings for 3 mins in batches of 5.
- Remove any excess oils by placing everything on some paper towels.
- Enjoy.

Amount per serving (15 total)

Timing Information:

Preparation	45 m
Cooking	25 m
Total Time	1 h 10 m

Nutritional Information:

Calories	168 kcal
Fat	10.5 g
Carbohydrates	11g
Protein	7 g
Cholesterol	23 mg
Sodium	288 mg

* Percent Daily Values are based on a 2,000 calorie diet.

HEALTHY VEGGIE BITES

Ingredients

- 20 thin slices sandwich bread, crusts removed, flattened with a rolling pin
- 3/4 lb butter
- 4 oz. blue cheese, at room temperature
- 1 (8 oz.) package cream cheese, at room temperature
- 1 egg, beaten
- 20 fresh asparagus spears

Directions

- Get a bowl, combine: egg, blue cheese, and cream cheese.
- Stir the mix until it is creamy then coat each piece of bread with the mix.
- Lay one asparagus on each piece of bread and roll everything together.
- Then stake a toothpick through each.
- Melt your butter and coat the wraps with the butter equally.
- Place everything on a cookie sheet or casserole dish and put everything in the freezer for 60 mins.
- Take out the toothpicks and slice each piece in half.
- Now set your oven to 400 degrees before doing anything else.
- Cook the wraps in the oven for 30 mins.
- Enjoy.

Amount per serving (10 total)

Timing Information:

Preparation	20 m
Cooking	25 m
Total Time	1 h 45 m

Nutritional Information:

Calories	463 kcal
Fat	40.3 g
Carbohydrates	18.6g
Protein	8.3 g
Cholesterol	125 mg
Sodium	651 mg

* Percent Daily Values are based on a 2,000 calorie diet.

TANGY CHEESE APPETIZER

Ingredients

- 6 tbsps butter
- 2 lbs medium fresh mushrooms, stems removed
- 1 (8 oz.) package Neufchatel cheese
- 1 (4 oz.) package goat cheese crumbles
- 2 tbsps finely chopped onion
- 1/2 C. mushroom stems, chopped
- 1/4 C. butter
- 1 tbsp finely chopped garlic

Directions

- Place 3 tbsps of butter in two frying pans and begin to fry half of your mushrooms in each one for 7 mins then place the mushrooms to the side.
- Get a bowl, combine: goat cheese, cream cheese, mushrooms stems, and onions.
- Stir the mix evenly then stuff your mushroom caps with the mix.
- Place everything in a broiler pan.
- Get 1/4 C. of butter melted then add in the garlic and cook everything for 60 secs then top the mushrooms with the garlic butter.
- Put everything in the broiler for 7 mins. Enjoy.

Amount per serving (6 total)

Timing Information:

Preparation	30 m
Cooking	15 m
Total Time	45 m

Nutritional Information:

Calories	373 kcal
Fat	34.1 g
Carbohydrates	7.5g
Protein	13 g
Cholesterol	94 mg
Sodium	391 mg

* Percent Daily Values are based on a 2,000 calorie diet.

Mediterranean Appetizer

Ingredients

- 2 (6 oz.) jars marinated artichoke hearts, divided
- 1 small onion, finely chopped
- 1 1/2 cloves garlic, minced
- 4 large eggs, beaten
- 1/4 C. dry bread crumbs
- 1/4 tsp salt
- 1/8 tsp ground black pepper
- 1/4 tsp dried oregano
- 1/2 tsp hot pepper sauce (such as Tabasco(R))
- 3/4 lb sharp Cheddar cheese, shredded
- 2 tbsps minced fresh parsley
- 1 tsp grated Parmesan cheese

Directions

- Coat a casserole dish with oil then set your oven to 325 degrees before doing anything else.
- Pour the liquid from 1 jar of the artichokes in a frying pan then place the pieces of artichokes and everything from the second jar into the bowl of a food processor.

- Process the mix until it is chopped then place everything to the side.
- Begin to stir fry your garlic and onions for 8 mins, in the artichoke liquid, then place everything in a bowl.
- Get a 2nd bowl, combine: hot sauce, onion mix, oregano, eggs, black pepper, bread crumbs, and salt.
- Add in the processed artichokes, cheddar, parmesan, and parsley.
- Place everything into the casserole dish and cook it all in the oven for 27 mins.
- Slice the dish into serving pieces.
- Enjoy.

Amount per serving (36 total)

Timing Information:

Preparation	30 m
Cooking	30 m
Total Time	1 h

Nutritional Information:

Calories	59 kcal
Fat	4.2 g
Carbohydrates	2g
Protein	< 3.5 g
Cholesterol	31 mg
Sodium	125 mg

* Percent Daily Values are based on a 2,000 calorie diet.

UPSTATE MAINE APPETIZER

Ingredients

- 3/4 C. white wine
- 3/4 C. tomato and clam juice cocktail
- 3 cloves garlic - peeled and sliced
- 1/2 tsp crushed red pepper flakes
- 1 lb mussels, cleaned and de-bearded
- 3 tbsps butter

Directions

- Get the following boiling in a large pan: pepper flakes, wine, garlic, and juice cocktail.
- Once the mix is boiling place a lid on the pot, and let everything cook for 7 mins. At this point all the mussels should no longer be closed.
- Any mussel that are closed should be thrown away.
- Place the opened mussels to the side then keep about 1 C. of the liquid and begin to boil it until about 25% of it has evaporated.
- Combine in the butter and let the mix get thicker.
- Top your mussels with the sauce.
- Enjoy.

Amount per serving (3 total)

Timing Information:

Preparation	10 m
Cooking	10 m
Total Time	20 m

Nutritional Information:

Calories	214 kcal
Fat	12 g
Carbohydrates	10.5g
Protein	5.3 g
Cholesterol	42 mg
Sodium	371 mg

* Percent Daily Values are based on a 2,000 calorie diet.

MEXICAN STYLE FESTIVE CHEESECAKES

Ingredients

- 2 C. crushed tortilla chips
- 2 tbsps butter, melted
- 3 (8 oz.) packages cream cheese, softened
- 1 1/4 C. shredded Colby cheese
- 8 oz. cottage cheese
- 4 eggs
- 4 oz. chopped green chile peppers
- 8 oz. jalapeno cheese dip
- 8 oz. sour cream
- 1 tomato, chopped
- 4 oz. sour cream
- 2 (2 oz.) cans sliced black olives
- 2 bunches green onions, chopped

Directions

- Set your oven to 350 degrees before doing anything else.
- Get a bowl, combine: melted butter and tortilla chips. Place everything into a spring form pan.

- Get a 2nd bowl, combine: chili pepper, cream cheese, eggs, Colby jack, and cottage cheese.
- Layer this mix over the chips in the spring form pan.
- Cook everything for 60 mins.
- Get a 3rd bowl, combine: sour cream and jalapeno dip. Then place this over the cottage cheese mix in the oven.
- Continue cooking everything for 12 more mins.
- Now let the dish sit for 5 hrs then add some sour cream on top and lay the green onions, black olives, and tomatoes around the dish.
- Enjoy.

Amount per serving (20 total)

Timing Information:

Preparation	20 m
Cooking	1 h 10 m
Total Time	5 h 50 m

Nutritional Information:

Calories	274 kcal
Fat	23.3 g
Carbohydrates	7.8g
Protein	8.9 g
Cholesterol	94 mg
Sodium	384 mg

* Percent Daily Values are based on a 2,000 calorie diet.

Gouda and Shrimp Cake

Ingredients

- 1 tbsp olive oil
- 1 onion
- 6 tsps minced garlic
- 1 lb fresh shrimp, peeled and deveined
- 12 shells puff pastry, baked
- 4 tbsps butter or margarine
- 3 (8 oz.) packages cream cheese, softened
- 4 eggs
- 1/2 C. heavy cream
- 16 oz. smoked Gouda, grated
- 2 tsps salt

Directions

- Set your oven to 350 degrees before doing anything else.
- Begin to stir fry your garlic and onions until the onions are see-through then place them to the side.
- Place 12 pieces of shrimp to the side and dice the rest into half inch pieces.
- Fry the shrimp for 5 mins.

- Get a bowl and begin to whisk your cream cheese until it is fluffy then add in your eggs 1 by one.
- Once the eggs are mixed in combine in the salt, cream, shrimp, Gouda, and onions.
- Enter this mix into your pastry shells and cook everything in the oven for 30 mins.
- Top the dish with some chives and the whole shrimp.
- Enjoy.

Amount per serving (12 total)

Timing Information:

Preparation	45 m
Cooking	25 m
Total Time	1 h 10 m

Nutritional Information:

Calories	701 kcal
Fat	56.3 g
Carbohydrates	22.7g
Protein	26.8 g
Cholesterol	248 mg
Sodium	1075 mg

* Percent Daily Values are based on a 2,000 calorie diet.

Mozzarella, Tomatoes, and Basil Appetizer

Ingredients

- 20 grape tomatoes
- 10 oz. mozzarella cheese, cubed
- 2 tbsps extra virgin olive oil
- 2 tbsps fresh basil leaves, chopped
- 1 pinch salt
- 1 pinch ground black pepper
- 20 toothpicks

Directions

- Get a bowl, combine: pepper, tomatoes, salt, mozzarella, basil, and olive oil.
- Stake your toothpicks with a piece of mozzarella and tomato.
- Enjoy.

Amount per serving (10 total)

Timing Information:

Preparation	
Cooking	15 m
Total Time	15 m

Nutritional Information:

Calories	104 kcal
Fat	7.3 g
Carbohydrates	2.4g
Protein	< 7.2 g
Cholesterol	18 mg
Sodium	179 mg

* Percent Daily Values are based on a 2,000 calorie diet.

Summer Soiree Shrimp

Ingredients

- 1 (8 oz.) package cream cheese, softened
- 2 tsps Worcestershire sauce
- 1 tsp hot pepper sauce
- 1 (8 oz.) jar cocktail sauce
- 2 (6 oz.) containers shrimp, rinsed and drained
- 2 chopped green onions
- 1 tomato, chopped
- 1/2 C. shredded mozzarella cheese

Directions

- Get a bowl, combine: hot sauce, Worcestershire, and cream cheese.
- Layer the mix on a dish for serving then layer your shrimp and cocktail sauce over everything before adding your mozzarella, tomato, and green onions.
- Enjoy.

Amount per serving (28 total)

Timing Information:

Preparation	
Cooking	10 m
Total Time	10 m

Nutritional Information:

Calories	56 kcal
Fat	3.4 g
Carbohydrates	2.3g
Protein	< 4 g
Cholesterol	31 mg
Sodium	159 mg

* Percent Daily Values are based on a 2,000 calorie diet.

JALAPENO JELLY SAUSAGE

Ingredients

- 1 lb kielbasa, cut into 1/4-inch slices
- 1 onion, chopped
- 1/2 C. mustard
- 1 (10 oz.) jar prepared jalapeno pepper jelly

Directions

- Add the following to the crock of a slow cooker: jalapeno jelly, kielbasa, mustard, and onions.
- Stir the mix then place a lid on the crock pot.
- Set the heat to high and let the mix cook for 40 mins.
- Enjoy.

Amount per serving (6 total)

Timing Information:

Preparation	10 m
Cooking	30 m
Total Time	40 m

Nutritional Information:

Calories	373 kcal
Fat	21.5 g
Carbohydrates	35.6g
Protein	10.4 g
Cholesterol	50 mg
Sodium	945 mg

* Percent Daily Values are based on a 2,000 calorie diet.

Pepper Tomatoes and Eggplant

Ingredients

- 5 eggplants, peeled and cubed
- 5 green bell peppers, seeded and chopped
- 5 tomatoes, chopped
- 5 onions, chopped
- 1 1/2 tbsps white sugar
- 1 tbsp salt
- 1/2 C. vegetable oil
- 1/2 C. red wine vinegar
- 1/2 C. water

Directions

- Add the following to a saucepan: onion, eggplant, tomato, and bell peppers.
- Get a bowl, combine: water, sugar, vinegar, salt, and oil.
- Stir the mix until it is smooth then add it to the saucepan as well.
- Get everything boiling then set the heat to a medium level and let the mix cook for 40 mins.
- Enjoy.

Amount per serving (48 total)

Timing Information:

Preparation	30 m
Cooking	30 m
Total Time	1 h

Nutritional Information:

Calories	43 kcal
Fat	2.4 g
Carbohydrates	5.4g
Protein	0.8 g
Cholesterol	0 mg
Sodium	148 mg

* Percent Daily Values are based on a 2,000 calorie diet.

BACON AND CHESTNUTS

Ingredients

- 1 (10 oz.) can whole chestnuts, drained
- 2 C. soy sauce
- 1 C. brown sugar
- 1 lb bacon

Directions

- Get a bowl, mix: soy sauce and chestnuts.
- Place a covering of plastic on the bowl and put everything in the fridge for 40 mins.
- Cover a casserole dish with foil.
- Coat it with nonstick spray then set your oven to 450 degrees before doing anything else.
- Cut your pieces of bacon into three pieces.
- Get a bowl for your brown sugar then dredge your chestnuts in the sugar and cover each chestnut with a piece of bacon.
- Place a tooth through each and put everything in the casserole dish.
- Cook the chestnuts in the oven until the bacon is fully done.
- Enjoy.

Amount per serving (15 total)

Timing Information:

Preparation	10 m
Cooking	50 m
Total Time	1 h

Nutritional Information:

Calories	230 kcal
Fat	13.9 g
Carbohydrates	20.5g
Protein	6 g
Cholesterol	21 mg
Sodium	2179 mg

* Percent Daily Values are based on a 2,000 calorie diet.

BREAD FOR CELEBRATIONS

Ingredients

- 1 (1 lb) loaf unsliced white bread
- 1 C. freshly grated Parmesan cheese
- 1 C. grated Romano cheese
- 6 cloves garlic, crushed
- 1/2 C. chopped fresh parsley
- 1 C. extra virgin olive oil
- 2 tbsps dried red chile peppers

Directions

- Set your oven to 300 degrees before doing anything else.
- Get a casserole dish and lay your pieces of bread in the dish.
- Cut out 8 slices only halfway down the piece of bread.
- Coat the bread with half of the olive oil, parmesan, parsley, Romano, and garlic.
- Layer your chili peppers around the bread and cook everything for 20 mins in the oven.
- Top the bread with the rest of the olive oil.
- Enjoy.

Amount per serving (8 total)

Timing Information:

Preparation	15 m
Cooking	15 m
Total Time	30 m

Nutritional Information:

Calories	510 kcal
Fat	36.8 g
Carbohydrates	31.1g
Protein	13.2 g
Cholesterol	24 mg
Sodium	721 mg

* Percent Daily Values are based on a 2,000 calorie diet.

2 Cheese Spinach Bake

Ingredients

- 1 (10 oz.) package frozen chopped spinach, thawed and drained
- 2 C. dry bread stuffing mix
- 3 eggs, beaten
- 1/4 C. grated Parmesan cheese
- 1/2 onion, chopped
- 2 tbsps melted butter
- 1/4 C. shredded Cheddar cheese

Directions

- Get a bowl, combine: cheddar, spinach, butter, stuffing mix, onion, eggs, and parmesan.
- Place a covering on the bowl and put everything in the fridge for 40 mins.
- Get a casserole dish and drop large dollops of the mix into the dish.
- Place everything in the freezer for 2 hrs.
- Now set your oven to 350 degrees before doing anything else and let the mix sit for 30 mins as the oven gets hot.
- Once the oven is hot cook the dollops for 30 mins.
- Enjoy.

Amount per serving (16 total)

Timing Information:

Preparation	20 m
Cooking	20 m
Total Time	2 h 40 m

Nutritional Information:

Calories	143 kcal
Fat	4.4 g
Carbohydrates	20.3g
Protein	5.7 g
Cholesterol	42 mg
Sodium	469 mg

* Percent Daily Values are based on a 2,000 calorie diet.

Zucchini and Romano Roast

Ingredients

- 1 C. baking mix
- 1/2 C. vegetable oil
- 2 tbsps dried parsley
- 1 pinch ground black pepper
- 2 cloves garlic, chopped
- 1 egg
- 1/2 C. grated Romano cheese
- 1/4 tsp salt
- 3 C. sliced zucchini

Directions

- Set your oven to 350 degrees before doing anything else.
- Get a bowl, combine: zucchini, baking mix, salt, veggie oil, Romano, parsley, egg, garlic, and pepper.
- Then place the mix into a casserole dish that has been coated with oil and cook everything in the oven for 25 mins.
- Slice the contents into serving pieces.
- Enjoy.

Amount per serving (40 total)

Timing Information:

Preparation	10 m
Cooking	20 m
Total Time	30 m

Nutritional Information:

Calories	46 kcal
Fat	3.7 g
Carbohydrates	2.3g
Protein	< 1 g
Cholesterol	6 mg
Sodium	73 mg

* Percent Daily Values are based on a 2,000 calorie diet.

Easy Appetizer Cookbook

Scallops for the Banquet

Ingredients

- 1 lb scallops, rinsed and patted dry, larger pieces cut in 4
- 1 C. French dressing
- 1/2 clove garlic, crushed

Directions

- Get a pot of water and salt boiling.
- Cook your scallops in it for 7 mins then remove all the liquids and add the scallops to a mason jar immediately.
- Now add in the garlic and French dressing.
- Place the lid on the jar tightly and shake everything.
- Place the scallops in the fridge until they are cold then layer everything onto a serving dish and stake a toothpick through each one.
- Enjoy.

Amount per serving (8 total)

Timing Information:

Preparation	5 m
Cooking	5 m
Total Time	10 m

Nutritional Information:

Calories	215 kcal
Fat	15.9 g
Carbohydrates	6.5g
Protein	9.5 g
Cholesterol	19 mg
Sodium	369 mg

* Percent Daily Values are based on a 2,000 calorie diet.

Sweet Beef Cocktails

Ingredients

- 1/4 C. milk
- 2 tbsps dried bread crumbs
- 1 tbsp minced onion
- 1/2 lb lean ground beef
- 2 tbsps water
- 2 tbsps soy sauce
- 1 tbsp vegetable oil
- 2 tsps white sugar
- 1/2 clove crushed garlic
- 1/4 tsp ground ginger

Directions

- Get a bowl, combine: ground beef, milk, chopped onions, and bread crumbs.
- Combine everything evenly then form the mix into 36 balls and layer them in a single casserole dish if they can fit or into two dishes.
- Get a 2nd bowl, combine: ginger, water, garlic, soy sauce, sugar, and veggie oil.
- Top your beef with the mix and leave everything for an hour covered in the fridge.

- Stir the mix then set your oven to 350 degrees before continuing.
- Cook everything in the oven for 30 mins.
- Enjoy.

Amount per serving (36 total)

Timing Information:

Preparation	20 m
Cooking	40 m
Total Time	1 h 10 m

Nutritional Information:

Calories	24 kcal
Fat	1.7 g
Carbohydrates	0.7g
Protein	< 1.3 g
Cholesterol	5 mg
Sodium	58 mg

* Percent Daily Values are based on a 2,000 calorie diet.

APRICOT AND BRIE PUFF PASTRY

Ingredients

- 1 (8 oz.) wheel Brie cheese
- 3 tbsps apricot preserves
- 1/2 (17.5 oz.) package frozen puff pastry, thawed
- 1 egg white

Directions

- Coat a casserole dish with oil then set your oven to 350 degrees before doing anything else.
- Cut your brie into two circular pieces then coat each with the preserves.
- Form the pieces into a sandwich and cover the sandwich with some puff pastry.
- Place the pastry onto a cookie sheet and top everything with egg whites.
- Cook the pastry for 35 mins in the oven.
- Enjoy.

Amount per serving (8 total)

Timing Information:

Preparation	10 m
Cooking	30 m
Total Time	40 m

Nutritional Information:

Calories	286 kcal
Fat	19.5 g
Carbohydrates	19.1g
Protein	8.6 g
Cholesterol	28 mg
Sodium	264 mg

* Percent Daily Values are based on a 2,000 calorie diet.

Mexican Appetizer

Ingredients

- 1 jicama, peeled and cut into bite-sized pieces
- 2 tbsps fresh lime juice
- 2 tbsps chili powder

Directions

- Lay out your jicama on a serving dish then top it with the chili powder and lime juice.
- Enjoy.

Amount per serving (4 total)

Timing Information:

Preparation	
Cooking	10 m
Total Time	10 m

Nutritional Information:

Calories	77 kcal
Fat	0.8 g
Carbohydrates	17.3g
Protein	1.7 g
Cholesterol	0 mg
Sodium	47 mg

* Percent Daily Values are based on a 2,000 calorie diet.

Easy Devils on Horseback

Ingredients

- 1 (8 oz.) package pitted dates
- 4 oz. almonds
- 1 lb sliced bacon

Directions

- Cut your dates in half then put an almond in each.
- Cover the dates with the bacon and stake a toothpick through each one.
- Place everything onto a broiler pan and cook the appetizers under the broiler for 12 mins.
- Enjoy.

Amount per serving (6 total)

Timing Information:

Preparation	30 m
Cooking	5 m
Total Time	35 m

Nutritional Information:

Calories	560 kcal
Fat	43.7 g
Carbohydrates	32.2g
Protein	13.7 g
Cholesterol	51 mg
Sodium	631 mg

* Percent Daily Values are based on a 2,000 calorie diet.

SPICY CHEESE APPETIZER

Ingredients

- 1 (8 oz.) package cream cheese, softened
- 1/2 C. mild pepper jelly

Directions

- Simply coat your cream cheese with the jelly and place everything on a serving platter.
- Slice the block of cheese into a strips and place toothpicks in each one.
- Enjoy.

Amount per serving (6 total)

Timing Information:

Preparation	
Cooking	2 m
Total Time	2 m

Nutritional Information:

Calories	197 kcal
Fat	13 g
Carbohydrates	18.5g
Protein	2.9 g
Cholesterol	41 mg
Sodium	118 mg

* Percent Daily Values are based on a 2,000 calorie diet.

CHINESE DUMPLINGS

Ingredients

- 1 (16 oz.) package wonton wrappers
- 1 lb beef sausage
- 1 C. shredded Monterey Jack cheese
- 1 C. shredded Cheddar cheese
- 1/2 C. chopped black olives, drained
- 1 C. Ranch-style salad dressing

Directions

- Coat a muffin tin with nonstick spray then set your oven to 350 degrees before doing anything else.
- Place your wonton wrappers in each section of the tin and cook them in the oven for 7 mins then place everything outside the oven to lose its heat.
- Get a bowl, combine: dressing, sausage, olives, cheddar, and Monterey.
- Divide the mix between the wrappers and cook everything for 13 more mins until the sausage is fully done.
- Enjoy.

Amount per serving (60 total)

Timing Information:

Preparation	15 m
Cooking	20 m
Total Time	35 m

Nutritional Information:

Calories	91 kcal
Fat	6.7 g
Carbohydrates	4.7g
Protein	2.7 g
Cholesterol	11 mg
Sodium	166 mg

* Percent Daily Values are based on a 2,000 calorie diet.

SPICY CHICKEN WINGS

Ingredients

- 1/2 C. all-purpose flour
- 1/4 tsp paprika
- 1/4 tsp cayenne pepper
- 1/4 tsp salt
- 10 chicken wings
- oil for deep frying
- 1/4 C. butter
- 1/4 C. hot sauce
- 1 dash ground black pepper
- 1 dash garlic powder

Directions

- Get a bowl, combine: salt, flour, cayenne, and paprika.
- Add in the chicken wings and evenly coat them.
- Place the wings in a separate bowl and place a covering of plastic on the bowl.
- Put everything in the fridge for 1.5 hours.
- Get your oil hot for frying in a deep pan.
- You want the wings to be fully submerged.
- Once the oil is hot fry the wings for 13 mins until golden and fully done then place the wings in a bowl and top everything with the hot sauce.
- Enjoy.

Amount per serving (5 total)

Timing Information:

Preparation	15 m
Cooking	15 m
Total Time	2 h

Nutritional Information:

Calories	364 kcal
Fat	32.4 g
Carbohydrates	10.7g
Protein	7.9 g
Cholesterol	44 mg
Sodium	497 mg

* Percent Daily Values are based on a 2,000 calorie diet.

Festive Bruschetta Appetizer

Ingredients

- 6 roma (plum) tomatoes, chopped
- 1/2 C. sun-dried tomatoes, packed in oil
- 3 cloves minced garlic
- 1/4 C. olive oil
- 2 tbsps balsamic vinegar
- 1/4 C. fresh basil, stems removed
- 1/4 tsp salt
- 1/4 tsp ground black pepper
- 1 French baguette
- 2 C. shredded mozzarella cheese

Directions

- Get your oven's broiler hot.
- Get a bowl, combine: pepper, roma tomatoes, salt, sun dried tomatoes, basil, garlic, vinegar, and olive oil.
- Stir the mix then leave it for 15 mins.
- Slice your bread into 1 inch pieces then place everything on a cookie sheet.
- Cook the pieces in the oven for 3 mins then equally top the pieces of bread with the tomato mix and a piece of mozzarella.
- Place the pieces of bread back in the broiler for 6 more mins.
- Enjoy.

Amount per serving (12 total)

Timing Information:

Preparation	15 m
Cooking	7 m
Total Time	35 m

Nutritional Information:

Calories	215 kcal
Fat	8.9 g
Carbohydrates	24.8g
Protein	9.6 g
Cholesterol	12 mg
Sodium	426 mg

* Percent Daily Values are based on a 2,000 calorie diet.

SPRINGTIME PARTY SHRIMP

Ingredients

- 3 cloves garlic, minced
- 1/3 C. olive oil
- 1/4 C. tomato sauce
- 2 tbsps red wine vinegar
- 2 tbsps chopped fresh basil
- 1/2 tsp salt
- 1/4 tsp cayenne pepper
- 2 lbs fresh shrimp, peeled and deveined
- skewers

Directions

- Get a bowl, combine: wine vinegar, garlic, tomato sauce, and olive oil.
- Combine in the cayenne, salt, and basil.
- Stir the mix then add in the shrimp and stir everything again.
- Place a covering of plastic on the bowl and put everything in the fridge for 60 mins.
- Now get a grill hot and coat the grate with oil.
- Place the shrimp on some skewers and grill everything for 4 mins each side.
- Enjoy.

Amount per serving (6 total)

Timing Information:

Preparation	15 m
Cooking	6 m
Total Time	55 m

Nutritional Information:

Calories	273 kcal
Fat	14.7 g
Carbohydrates	2.8g
Protein	< 31 g
Cholesterol	230 mg
Sodium	472 mg

* Percent Daily Values are based on a 2,000 calorie diet.

CUTE LITTLE SWEET SAUSAGES

Ingredients

- 1 lb sliced bacon, each piece cut into 3 pieces
- 1 (16 oz.) package little beef sausages
- 1 C. brown sugar, or to taste

Directions

- Set your oven to 350 degrees before doing anything else.
- Cover each sausage with a piece of bacon then top everything with the sugar.
- Place each piece on a skewer and then on a cookie sheet.
- Cook the appetizers in the oven until the bacon is fully done.
- Enjoy.

Amount per serving (12 total)

Timing Information:

Preparation	10 m
Cooking	20 m
Total Time	30 m

Nutritional Information:

Calories	356 kcal
Fat	27.2 g
Carbohydrates	18.9g
Protein	9 g
Cholesterol	49 mg
Sodium	696 mg

* Percent Daily Values are based on a 2,000 calorie diet.

Rustic Cheddar and Onion Baguette

Ingredients

- 1 C. mayonnaise
- 1 C. shredded aged Cheddar cheese
- 3/4 C. finely chopped slivered almonds
- 6 slices crisply cooked bacon, crumbled
- 2 green onions, finely chopped, or more to taste
- 2 tsps Worcestershire sauce
- 1 loaf baguette, cut into 1- to 2-inch slices

Directions

- Set your oven to 375 degrees before doing anything else.
- Get a bowl, combine: Worcestershire, mayo, green onions, cheddar, bacon, and almonds.
- Divide the mix between your pieces of bread and place everything on a cookie sheet.
- Cook everything in the oven for 9 mins.
- Enjoy.

Amount per serving (12 total)

Timing Information:

Preparation	15 m
Cooking	10 m
Total Time	25 m

Nutritional Information:

Calories	338 kcal
Fat	23.1 g
Carbohydrates	23.8g
Protein	9.5 g
Cholesterol	20 mg
Sodium	488 mg

* Percent Daily Values are based on a 2,000 calorie diet.

Parmesan Rolls

Ingredients

- 1 (8 oz.) package Cream Cheese, softened
- 8 slices Bacon, cooked, crumbled
- 1/3 C. Grated Parmesan Cheese
- 1/4 C. finely chopped onions
- 2 tbsps chopped fresh parsley
- 1 tbsp milk
- 2 (8 oz.) packages refrigerated crescent dinner rolls

Directions

- Get a bowl, combine: cream cheese, bacon, parmesan, onion, parsley, and milk.
- Combine the mix until it is smooth.
- Break your pieces of dough into eight triangles then cut each piece in half.
- Top each piece with 1 tsp of mix and roll it up.
- Lay everything onto a cookie sheet and cook it all in the oven for 14 mins.
- Enjoy.

Amount per serving (16 total)

Timing Information:

Preparation	
Cooking	20 m
Total Time	35 m

Nutritional Information:

Calories	170 kcal
Fat	11.5 g
Carbohydrates	12.2g
Protein	4.4 g
Cholesterol	20 mg
Sodium	353 mg

* Percent Daily Values are based on a 2,000 calorie diet.

APPLES AND BEEF

Ingredients

- 2 lbs beef sausage
- 3/4 C. packed brown sugar
- 1 C. chunky applesauce
- 1 onion, chopped

Directions

- Set your oven to 325 degrees before doing anything else.
- Begin to fry your sausage until it is fully done then cut it into pieces.
- Get a baking dish then stir the following in it: onion, sausage, applesauce, and brown sugar.
- Cook everything in the oven for 50 mins.
- Enjoy.

Amount per serving (8 total)

Timing Information:

Preparation	10 m
Cooking	45 m
Total Time	55 m

Nutritional Information:

Calories	501 kcal
Fat	35.6 g
Carbohydrates	28.6g
Protein	16.4 g
Cholesterol	86 mg
Sodium	837 mg

* Percent Daily Values are based on a 2,000 calorie diet.

BACON WRAPPER

Ingredients

- 12 fresh chicken livers, halved
- 1 tsp garlic salt
- 12 slices bacon, cut in half

Directions

- Get your oven's broiler hot.
- Coat each piece of liver with garlic salt then cover each with a piece of bacon.
- Stake a toothpick through each and layer everything into a broiler dish.
- Cook the livers under the broiler for 6 mins then flip the pieces and continue to broil them for 6 more mins.
- Enjoy.

Amount per serving (24 total)

Timing Information:

Preparation	5 m
Cooking	15 m
Total Time	20 m

Nutritional Information:

Calories	83 kcal
Fat	7.1 g
Carbohydrates	0.1g
Protein	< 4.3 g
Cholesterol	65 mg
Sodium	203 mg

* Percent Daily Values are based on a 2,000 calorie diet.

Caprese Sandwiches

Ingredients

- 24 long cocktail toothpicks
- 48 cherry or grape tomatoes, rinsed and dried
- 6 thin slices prosciutto, each cut into quarters, folded into squares
- 24 bite-size marinated mozzarella balls*
- 24 fresh basil leaves
- 1/4 C. Italian salad dressing

Directions

- Stake the following on each toothpick: piece of folded prosciutto, piece of folded basil, one tomato, one mozzarella piece, and another tomato.
- Place everything on a dish and top it with dressing.
- Enjoy.

Amount per serving (6 total)

Timing Information:

Preparation	
Cooking	20 m
Total Time	20 m

Nutritional Information:

Calories	312 kcal
Fat	22.6 g
Carbohydrates	10.2g
Protein	19.8 g
Cholesterol	63 mg
Sodium	683 mg

* Percent Daily Values are based on a 2,000 calorie diet.

Festive Sandwich

Ingredients

- 1 C. butter, softened
- 3 tbsps poppy seeds
- 1 onion, grated
- 1 tbsp Worcestershire sauce
- 2 tbsps prepared Dijon-style mustard
- 2 (12 oz.) packages white party rolls
- 1/2 lb chopped cooked ham
- 5 oz. shredded Swiss cheese

Directions

- Set your oven to 350 degrees before doing anything else.
- Get a bowl, combine: Dijon, butter, Worcestershire, poppy seeds, and onions.
- Cut your bread into 2 pieces then coat each piece with the mix.
- Place a piece of cheese and some ham equally then place everything into a casserole dish.
- Cook the rolls in the oven for 13 mins.
- Enjoy.

Amount per serving (12 total)

Timing Information:

Preparation	15 m
Cooking	12 m
Total Time	30 m

Nutritional Information:

Calories	416 kcal
Fat	27.2 g
Carbohydrates	31.4g
Protein	12.1 g
Cholesterol	63 mg
Sodium	748 mg

* Percent Daily Values are based on a 2,000 calorie diet.

COUNTRYSIDE SAUSAGE APPETIZER

Ingredients

- 3 C. biscuit baking mix
- 1 lb bulk pork sausage
- 4 C. shredded Cheddar cheese
- 1/2 C. grated Parmesan cheese
- 1/2 C. milk
- 1 1/2 tsps dried parsley

Directions

- Coat a broiler pan with oil then set your oven to 350 degrees before doing anything else.
- Get a bowl, combine: parsley, sausage, milk, baking mix, parmesan, and cheddar.
- Work the mix evenly with your hands then shape everything into balls.
- Place the meat into the pan and cook them under the broiler for 30 mins.
- Check to make sure nothing burns and turn the balls at least twice as they cook.
- Enjoy.

Amount per serving (10 total)

Timing Information:

Preparation	15 m
Cooking	25 m
Total Time	40 m

Nutritional Information:

Calories	468 kcal
Fat	31.6 g
Carbohydrates	23.9g
Protein	21.9 g
Cholesterol	78 mg
Sodium	1206 mg

* Percent Daily Values are based on a 2,000 calorie diet.

Chinese Party Wontons

Ingredients

- 100 (3.5 inch square) wonton wrappers
- 1 3/4 lbs ground beef
- 1 tbsp minced fresh ginger root
- 4 cloves garlic, minced
- 2 tbsps thinly sliced green onion
- 4 tbsps soy sauce
- 3 tbsps sesame oil
- 1 egg, beaten
- 5 C. finely shredded Chinese cabbage

Directions

- Get a bowl, combine: cabbage, beef, egg, ginger, sesame oil, garlic, soy sauce, and green onions.
- Lay out your wonton wrappers and add 1 tsp of mix to each.
- Form each wrapper into a dumpling then steam the dumpling with a steamer insert over 2 inches of boiling water or a steamer basket.
- Let the dumplings steam for 25 mins until the meat is fully done.
- Enjoy.

Amount per serving (6 total)

Timing Information:

Preparation	30 m
Cooking	30 m
Total Time	1 h

Nutritional Information:

Calories	752 kcal
Fat	28.8 g
Carbohydrates	81.1g
Protein	39.2 g
Cholesterol	129 mg
Sodium	1449 mg

* Percent Daily Values are based on a 2,000 calorie diet.

Creamy Salmon and Tomatoes

Ingredients

- 50 cherry tomatoes, cleaned, dried, tops and bottoms removed
- 1 (8 oz.) package cream cheese, softened
- 2 oz. smoked salmon, finely chopped
- 2 1/2 tbsps heavy cream
- 3 drops lemon juice
- ground black pepper to taste

Directions

- Take out the insides of your tomatoes and put the tomato insides in a bowl.
- Get a 2nd bowl, combine: black pepper, cream cheese, lemon juice, salmon, and cream.
- Use a mixer for 3 mins then add the mix to a cookie press.
- Place the mix into the tomatoes.
- Enjoy.

Amount per serving (25 total)

Timing Information:

Preparation	
Cooking	35 m
Total Time	35 m

Nutritional Information:

Calories	46 kcal
Fat	3.9 g
Carbohydrates	1.9g
Protein	< 1.4 g
Cholesterol	12 mg
Sodium	48 mg

* Percent Daily Values are based on a 2,000 calorie diet.

Appetizers for March

Ingredients

- 4 eggs
- 2 tbsps cream cheese
- 2 tbsps chopped onion
- 2 tbsps minced cooked ham
- 1/4 C. seasoned bread crumbs

Directions

- Set your oven to 400 degrees before doing anything else.
- Get your eggs boiling in water.
- Once the eggs are boiling, place a lid on the pot, shut the heat, and leave the eggs for 15 mins.
- Drain out the water and remove the shells of the eggs.
- Slice them in half and take out the yolks.
- Get a bowl, mix: ham, onion, and cream cheese.
- Enter the mix into the eggs and layer them in a casserole dish.
- Cook the eggs in the oven for 7 mins.
- Enjoy.

Amount per serving (4 total)

Timing Information:

Preparation	10 m
Cooking	15 m
Total Time	25 m

Nutritional Information:

Calories	138 kcal
Fat	8.7 g
Carbohydrates	6.2g
Protein	8.7 g
Cholesterol	196 mg
Sodium	278 mg

* Percent Daily Values are based on a 2,000 calorie diet.

CRESCENTS AND CHEESE

Ingredients

- 1/2 (8 oz.) package refrigerated crescent rolls
- 1 (8 oz.) package cream cheese
- 1/2 tsp dried dill weed
- 1 egg yolk, beaten

Directions

- Set your oven to 350 degrees before doing anything else.
- Lay out your dough on a cutting board coated with flour.
- Take your cream cheese and coat one side of it with half of the dill weeds then lay the dill side of the cheese facing downwards on the dough and top the other side with the rest of the dill.
- Lay the dough over the cheese and crimp the edge to form a seal.
- Coat a baking sheet with oil and place the dough on the sheet and cook everything in the oven for 17 mins.
- Enjoy.

Amount per serving (8 total)

Timing Information:

Preparation	10 m
Cooking	20 m
Total Time	30 m

Nutritional Information:

Calories	159 kcal
Fat	13.3 g
Carbohydrates	6.4g
Protein	3.5 g
Cholesterol	56 mg
Sodium	194 mg

* Percent Daily Values are based on a 2,000 calorie diet.

Basil Zucchini Bites

Ingredients

- 8 tbsps grated Parmesan cheese
- 1/2 C. vegetable oil
- 1/2 C. sesame seeds
- 1 onion, chopped
- 1 clove garlic, minced
- 2 1/2 C. grated zucchini
- 6 eggs, beaten
- 1/3 C. dried bread crumbs
- 1/2 tsp salt
- 1/2 tsp dried basil
- 1/2 tsp dried oregano
- 1/4 tsp ground black pepper
- 3 C. shredded Cheddar cheese

Directions

- Coat a casserole dish with oil and with 3 tbsp of parmesan.
- Then set your oven to 325 degrees before doing anything else.
- Begin to toast your sesame seeds in half a tsp of veggie oil.
- Get a bowl, combine: cheddar, veggie oil, pepper, onion, oregano, garlic, basil, zucchini, salt, eggs, and bread crumbs.
- Combine the mix until it is even then layer everything into the casserole dish.
- Top the mix with the sesame seeds and parmesan.
- Cook the dish in the oven for 35 mins.
- Then cut it into servings once it has cooled off.
- Enjoy.

Amount per serving (10 total)

Timing Information:

Preparation	5 m
Cooking	30 m
Total Time	55 m

Nutritional Information:

Calories	359 kcal
Fat	30.2 g
Carbohydrates	7.3g
Protein	16 g
Cholesterol	151 mg
Sodium	460 mg

* Percent Daily Values are based on a 2,000 calorie diet.

SWEET PEAS

Ingredients

- 1 lb sugar snap peas, trimmed
- 3 tbsps garlic flavored olive oil
- 1/4 C. low sodium soy sauce
- 1/4 tsp sesame oil
- 2 drops chili oil
- 1/4 tsp packed brown sugar
- 2 tbsps toasted sesame seeds

Directions

- Get your oven's broiler hot.
- Get a broiler pan and lay your snap peas in it then top them with the olive oil.
- Cook the peas under the broiler for 7 mins.
- At the same time get a bowl, combine: sesame seeds, soy sauce, brown sugar, sesame oil, and chili oil.
- Top your peas evenly with the oil mix when they are finish cooking.
- Enjoy.

Amount per serving (4 total)

Timing Information:

Preparation	15 m
Cooking	5 m
Total Time	20 m

Nutritional Information:

Calories	184 kcal
Fat	12.9 g
Carbohydrates	12.3g
Protein	4.4 g
Cholesterol	0 mg
Sodium	532 mg

* Percent Daily Values are based on a 2,000 calorie diet.

NEW YORK STYLE PIZZA BITES

Ingredients

- 1 C. prepared spinach dip
- 1 (10 oz.) package prepared pizza crust
- 1 C. chopped broccoli
- 1 C. cooked and cubed chicken
- 1/3 C. chopped green onions
- 1 tomato, seeded and chopped

Directions

- Coat your pizza crust with the spinach dip mix then layer your tomato, broccoli, green onions, and chicken over it.
- Slice the pizza into slices then place them on a serving dish.
- Enjoy.

Amount per serving (8 total)

Timing Information:

Preparation	
Cooking	5 m
Total Time	5 m

Nutritional Information:

Calories	306 kcal
Fat	19.5 g
Carbohydrates	22.7g
Protein	10.3 g
Cholesterol	30 mg
Sodium	439 mg

* Percent Daily Values are based on a 2,000 calorie diet.

Little Japanese Meatballs

Ingredients

- 2 tbsps minced onion
- 1/4 C. Kikkoman Teriyaki Marinade & Sauce
- 2 lbs lean ground beef
- 1 C. Kikkoman Panko Bread Crumbs
- Kikkoman Teriyaki Baste & Glaze

Directions

- Set your oven to 325 degrees before doing anything else.
- Get a bowl, combine: ground beef, onion, panko, and teriyaki.
- Work the mix with your hands then form everything into little meatballs.
- Lay the appetizers on a cookie sheet and cook them in the oven for 25 mins.
- Enjoy.

Amount per serving (12 total)

Timing Information:

Preparation	10 m
Cooking	40 m
Total Time	50 m

Nutritional Information:

Calories	185 kcal
Fat	9.7 g
Carbohydrates	6.7g
Protein	16.5 g
Cholesterol	52 mg
Sodium	382 mg

* Percent Daily Values are based on a 2,000 calorie diet.

PIMENTOS AND BLUE CHEESE

Ingredients

- 1 large cucumber
- 1 (3 oz.) package cream cheese, softened
- 1/4 C. blue cheese salad dressing
- 1 (1 lb) loaf cocktail rye bread
- 15 pimento-stuffed green olives, chopped

Directions

- Perforate your cucumber with a fork then cut it into slices.
- Get a bowl, combine: blue cheese and cream cheese.
- Top your pieces of bread with the cheese mix then equally with the cucumber and some olives.
- Enjoy.

Amount per serving (10 total)

Timing Information:

Preparation	
Cooking	5 m
Total Time	5 m

Nutritional Information:

Calories	190 kcal
Fat	8.7 g
Carbohydrates	23.1g
Protein	5.3 g
Cholesterol	11 mg
Sodium	507 mg

* Percent Daily Values are based on a 2,000 calorie diet.

Authentic Guacamole

Ingredients

- 3 avocados - peeled, pitted, and mashed
- 1 lime, juiced
- 1 tsp salt
- 1/2 C. minced onion
- 3 tbsps chopped fresh cilantro
- 2 roma (plum) tomatoes, minced
- 1 tsp minced garlic
- 1 pinch ground cayenne pepper (optional)

Directions

- Get a bowl, combine: salt, avocadoes, and lime juice.
- Mash everything together evenly then combine in: the garlic, onions, tomatoes, and cilantro.
- Stir the mix again then combine in the cayenne.
- Place a covering of plastic on the bowl and put everything in the fridge for 65 mins.
- Enjoy.

Amount per serving (4 total)

Timing Information:

Preparation	
Cooking	10 m
Total Time	10 m

Nutritional Information:

Calories	262 kcal
Fat	22.2 g
Carbohydrates	18g
Protein	3.7 g
Cholesterol	0 mg
Sodium	596 mg

* Percent Daily Values are based on a 2,000 calorie diet.

Jalapeno Bites

Ingredients

- 2 (8 oz.) packages cream cheese, softened
- 1 C. mayonnaise
- 1 (4 oz.) can chopped green chilies, drained
- 2 oz. canned minced jalapeno peppers, drained
- 1 C. grated Parmesan cheese

Directions

- Get a bowl, combine: mayo and cream cheese.
- Combine in the jalapeno pepper and green chilies.
- Combine the mix until it is smooth then add in the parmesan.
- Place everything in the microwave for 4 mins with the highest level of heat.
- Enjoy.

Amount per serving (32 total)

Timing Information:

Preparation	10 m
Cooking	3 m
Total Time	13 m

Nutritional Information:

Calories	110 kcal
Fat	11.1 g
Carbohydrates	1g
Protein	< 2.1 g
Cholesterol	20 mg
Sodium	189 mg

* Percent Daily Values are based on a 2,000 calorie diet.

Toasted Party Pecans

Ingredients

- 1 egg white
- 1 tbsp water
- 1 lb pecan halves
- 1 C. white sugar
- 3/4 tsp salt
- 1/2 tsp ground cinnamon

Directions

- Coat one cookie sheet with nonstick spray then set your oven to 250 degrees before doing anything else.
- Get a bowl, combine: water and egg whites.
- Whisk the mix until it is frothy.
- Then add in the pecans and whisk the mix again.
- Get a 2nd bowl, combine: cinnamon, sugar, and salt.
- Place the pecans in the sugar mix then place everything onto the cookie sheet.
- Cook the pecans for 65 mins and stir the nuts at least 3 times as they cook.
- Enjoy.

Amount per serving (12 total)

Timing Information:

Preparation	10 m
Cooking	1 h 10 m
Total Time	1 h 20 m

Nutritional Information:

Calories	328 kcal
Fat	27.2 g
Carbohydrates	22g
Protein	3.8 g
Cholesterol	0 mg
Sodium	150 mg

* Percent Daily Values are based on a 2,000 calorie diet.

Red and Green Salad

Ingredients

- 2 bunches spinach, rinsed and torn into bite-size pieces
- 4 C. sliced strawberries
- 1/2 C. vegetable oil
- 1/4 C. white wine vinegar
- 1/2 C. white sugar
- 1/4 tsp paprika
- 2 tbsps sesame seeds
- 1 tbsp poppy seeds

Directions

- Get a bowl, combine: strawberries and spinach.
- Get a 2nd bowl, combine: poppy seeds, oil, sesame seeds, vinegar, paprika, and sugar.
- Top the spinach with this mix and stir everything.
- Enjoy.

Amount per serving (8 total)

Timing Information:

Preparation	
Cooking	10 m
Total Time	10 m

Nutritional Information:

Calories	235 kcal
Fat	15.9 g
Carbohydrates	22.8g
Protein	3.6 g
Cholesterol	0 mg
Sodium	69 mg

* Percent Daily Values are based on a 2,000 calorie diet.

Mediterranean Pitas

Ingredients

- 1 (6 oz.) tub sun-dried tomato pesto
- 6 (6 inch) whole wheat pita breads
- 2 roma (plum) tomatoes, chopped
- 1 bunch spinach, rinsed and chopped
- 4 fresh mushrooms, sliced
- 1/2 C. crumbled feta cheese
- 2 tbsps grated Parmesan cheese
- 3 tbsps olive oil
- ground black pepper to taste

Directions

- Set your oven to 350 degrees before doing anything else.
- Coat your pieces of pita with tomato pesto and lay the pieces on a cookie sheet with the pesto facing upwards.
- Layer your parmesan, tomatoes, feta, mushrooms, and spinach on top of the pesto and top everything with some pepper, salt, and olive oil.
- Cook the pitas in the oven for 15 mins.
- Enjoy.

Amount per serving (6 total)

Timing Information:

Preparation	10 m
Cooking	12 m
Total Time	22 m

Nutritional Information:

Calories	350 kcal
Fat	17.1 g
Carbohydrates	41.6g
Protein	11.6 g
Cholesterol	13 mg
Sodium	587 mg

* Percent Daily Values are based on a 2,000 calorie diet.

Catalina's Cuban Sandwich

Ingredients

- 1 C. mayonnaise
- 5 tbsps Italian dressing
- 4 hoagie rolls, split lengthwise
- 4 tbsps prepared mustard
- 1/2 lb thinly sliced deli turkey meat
- 1/2 lb thinly sliced cooked ham
- 1/2 lb thinly sliced Swiss cheese
- 1 C. dill pickle slices
- 1/2 C. olive oil

Directions

- Get a bowl, combine: Italian dressing and mayo. Coat your bread liberally with the mix.
- Now add a layer of mustard then: cheese, ham, and turkey.
- Place some pickles across the sandwich and top the bread with olive oil.
- Fry the sandwiches for 3 mins each side and flatten the sandwich with a spatula as it cooks.
- Slice the sandwich into 2 pieces then serve.
- Enjoy.

NOTE: Cut the sandwich into small pieces and place everything onto a serving platter.

Amount per serving (4 total)

Timing Information:

Preparation	10 m
Cooking	12 m
Total Time	30 m

Nutritional Information:

Calories	1096 kcal
Fat	84.4 g
Carbohydrates	144.1g
Protein	43.3 g
Cholesterol	127 mg
Sodium	3110 mg

* Percent Daily Values are based on a 2,000 calorie diet.

Deviled Eggs Japanese Style

(デビルド卵)

Ingredients

- 9 eggs
- 2 tbsps sesame seeds
- 1/2 cup mayonnaise
- 2 tsps soy sauce
- 2 tsps wasabi paste
- 2 tsps rice wine vinegar
- 2 tbsps thinly sliced green onions
- 4 tbsps panko bread crumbs

Directions

- Boil your eggs in a saucepan. Once the water is boiling let it continue about 10 to 15 mins. Drain the water and run cold water over your eggs.
- Remove the shells. Place the eggs to the side.
- Get a frying pan and fry some sesame seeds for 4 mins. Set seeds aside.
- Split your shelled eggs and remove the yolks.
- Get your food processor and process the following until smooth: egg yolks, rice vinegar, mayo, wasabi paste and soy sauce.
- Put in some bread crumbs and green onion and pulse it a few more times.

- Put the processed contents into the center of your eggs and garnish each egg with sesame seeds.
- Enjoy.

Amount per serving: 18

Timing Information:

Preparation	30 m
Cooking	15 m
Total Time	55 m

Nutritional Information:

Calories	91 kcal
Carbohydrates	2.1 g
Cholesterol	95 mg
Fat	7.9 g
Fiber	0.1 g
Protein	3.6 g
Sodium	122 mg

* Percent Daily Values are based on a 2,000 calorie diet.

Rosemary Olive Tapas

INGREDIENTS

- 1 pint good green olives (or both mixed) or 1 pint black olives (or both mixed)
- 1/4 tsp kosher salt
- 1/2 tsp black peppercorns
- 3 bay leaves
- 3 sprigs fresh rosemary or 3 sprigs fresh thyme
- 1/2 tsp fennel seed, lightly crushed
- 4 -5 garlic cloves, cut in half lengthwise
- 1 pinch dried red pepper flakes (optional)
- 2 medium lemons, zested
- 3 tbsp extra virgin olive oil

Directions

- In a bowl, add all the ingredients and mix till well combined.
- Transfer into an airtight jar and refrigerate for about 12-24 hours.

Amount per serving: 4

Timing Information:

Preparation	10 mins
Total Time	12 hrs 10 mins

Nutritional Information:

Calories	201.7
Fat	20.5g
Cholesterol	0.0mg
Sodium	1156.0mg
Carbohydrates	6.6g
Protein	1.2g

* Percent Daily Values are based on a 2,000 calorie diet.

Nutty Brie and Bread

INGREDIENTS

- 1 baguette bread, cut into 20 slices
- 20 tsp olive oil
- ½ lb brie cheese
- 10 tsp honey
- 20 walnuts

Directions

- Set your oven to 300 degrees F before doing anything else.
- Cut each bread slice with oil evenly.
- Place 1 Brie cheese slice over each bread slice.
- Spread honey over each slice evenly and top with walnut halves.
- Cook in the oven for about 4 minutes

Amount per serving: 10

Timing Information:

Preparation	20 mins
Total Time	25 mins

Nutritional Information:

Calories	533.2
Fat	23.1g
Cholesterol	25.0mg
Sodium	683.4mg
Carbohydrates	64.7g
Protein	18.4g

* Percent Daily Values are based on a 2,000 calorie diet.

Barcelona Style Almonds

INGREDIENTS

- 1 tbsp coarse salt
- 1/2 tsp paprika (Spanish smoked)
- 1 lb almonds, blanched
- 1 -3 tbsp olive oil

Directions

- Set your oven to 400 degrees F before doing anything else.
- In a mortar and pestle or a coffee grinder, grind the salt and paprika till fine.
- In a cookie sheet, place the almonds and cook in the oven for about 5-10 minutes.
- Transfer the almonds in a bowl with oil and seasoning and toss to coat.

Amount per serving: 6

Timing Information:

Preparation	15 mins
Total Time	25 mins

Nutritional Information:

Calories	472.4
Fat	41.8g
Cholesterol	0.0mg
Sodium	1420.4mg
Carbohydrates	16.2g
Protein	16.0g

* Percent Daily Values are based on a 2,000 calorie diet.

Spicy Sherry Mushrooms
(Champinones Al Ajillo)

INGREDIENTS

- 3 tbsp extra virgin olive oil (Spanish preferred)
- 1/2 lb medium mushroom, stemmed, quartered
- 4 -6 garlic cloves, peeled and thinly sliced
- 2 -3 tsp fresh lemon juice
- 2 tbsp dry sherry
- 1/4 C. vegetable broth
- 1/2 tsp Spanish paprika
- 1/4 tsp crushed red pepper flakes
- salt, to taste
- fresh ground black pepper, to taste
- 1 tbsp fresh flat leaf parsley
- 2 lemon slices

Directions

- In a large skillet, heat the oil and sauté the mushrooms for about 1 minute.
- Add the garlic and sauté for about 1-2 minutes.
- Add the remaining ingredients except the parsley and lemon slices and simmer for about 2 minutes.
- Serve with a garnishing of the parsley alongside the lemon slices.

Amount per serving: 2

Timing Information:

Preparation	5 mins
Total Time	10 mins

Nutritional Information:

Calories	230.9
Fat	20.7g
Cholesterol	0.0mg
Sodium	9.5mg
Carbohydrates	7.5g
Protein	4.1g

* Percent Daily Values are based on a 2,000 calorie diet.

Garlic Potatoes

INGREDIENTS

- 3/4 lb salad potatoes
- 1/2 C. mayonnaise
- 3 garlic cloves, mashed to a paste or put through a garlic press
- 2 tbsp parsley, minced
- salt

Directions

- In a pan of salted water, cook the potato till tender and then drain them.
- Peel the potatoes and cut into 3/4-inch chunks.
- In a bowl, mix together the mayonnaise, parsley, garlic and salt.
- Fold in the potato chunks and serve.

Amount per serving: 4

Timing Information:

Preparation	10 mins
Total Time	20 mins

Nutritional Information:

Calories	184.1
Fat	9.9g
Cholesterol	7.6mg
Sodium	215.4mg
Carbohydrates	22.7g
Protein	2.1g

* Percent Daily Values are based on a 2,000 calorie diet.

CLASSICAL SPANISH TOMATO TAPAS

INGREDIENTS

- 4 slices French bread
- 2 ripe tomatoes, halved
- 1 garlic clove, finely chopped
- 2 tbsp Spanish olive oil

Directions

- Set the broiler of your oven.
- Cook the bread slices under the broiler till golden brown from both sides.
- Rub each halved tomato over 1 bread slice evenly.
- Sprinkle with the garlic evenly and serve with a drizzling of the oil.

Amount per serving: 4

Timing Information:

Preparation	10 mins
Total Time	12 mins

Nutritional Information:

Calories	196.0
Fat	1.2g
Cholesterol	0.0mg
Sodium	331.4mg
Carbohydrates	38.5g
Protein	8.0g

* Percent Daily Values are based on a 2,000 calorie diet.

Sausage Empanada

INGREDIENTS

- 1/2 C. chopped onion
- 1 garlic clove, minced
- 1/2 link hot linguica sausage, removed the casings and chopped
- 1/4 C. chopped bell pepper
- 3/4 tsp smoked paprika
- 1 small yellow wax chili pepper, seeded and minced
- 1 small tomatoes, seeded and chopped
- 1 (15 oz.) packages refrigerated pie crusts
- 1 egg, beaten

Directions

- Set your oven to 400 degrees F before doing anything else and line 2 baking sheets with the parchment papers.
- In a large skillet, heat the oil on medium heat and sauté the onion and garlic for about 10 minutes.
- Add the remaining ingredients except the egg and pie crust and increase the heat to medium-high heat.
- Cook for about 5 minutes.
- Unroll the pie crust and with a 3-inch cutter, cut into circles.

- Combine the scraps and roll and cut into circles on a lightly floured board.
- Place about spoonful of meat mixture onto half of each dough circle.
- With wet fingers, fold over to enclose filling and pinch edges to seal.
- Arrange onto prepared baking sheets and coat with the beaten egg.
- Cook in the oven for about 20-25 minutes.

Amount per serving: 1

Timing Information:

Preparation	20 mins
Total Time	1 hr

Nutritional Information:

Calories	83.0
Fat	5.1g
Cholesterol	7.5mg
Sodium	101.1mg
Carbohydrates	8.1g
Protein	0.9g

* Percent Daily Values are based on a 2,000 calorie diet.

Fish and Chips in Spain

INGREDIENTS

- 1 1/4 lbs salt cod fish
- 5 C. unsalted potatoes (riced or finely mashed)
- 1/2 C. finely chopped onion
- 1/3 C. finely chopped fresh parsley
- 4 tsp lemon juice
- 1/4 tsp nutmeg
- 1/4 tsp pepper
- 3 eggs, beaten
- oil (for deep frying)

Directions

- Rinse and soak the cod for about 12 hours or overnight in several changes of cold water, then drain well
- In a pan of water, add the cod and bring to a boil.
- Simmer for about 15 minutes and drain well, then keep aside to cool completely.
- Discard the skin and bones.
- In a food processor, add the cod and pulse till shredded finely.

- In a bowl, add the shredded cod and remaining ingredients except the oil and mix till well combined.
- With a dessert spoon, place a heaping spoon full of cod mixture.
- With a second dessert spoon place the mixture over the first press and form a rounded oval allowing excess to fall back into the bowl.
- Arrange onto a large tray and repeat with the remaining mixture.
- Serve alongside the lemon and olives.

Amount per serving: 1

Timing Information:

Preparation	13 hrs
Total Time	13 hrs 45 mins

Nutritional Information:

Calories	41.4
Fat	0.4g
Cholesterol	23.6mg
Sodium	669.7mg
Carbohydrates	2.3g
Protein	6.5g

* Percent Daily Values are based on a 2,000 calorie diet.

Classic Dijon Potato Tapas

INGREDIENTS

- 3 lbs potatoes, peeled and cut into 1 inch cubes
- 1 tbsp Dijon mustard
- 1/3 C. mayonnaise
- 2 garlic cloves, finely chopped
- 1 tbsp fresh thyme, finely chopped
- 1 tsp black pepper (freshly ground)
- 1/4 C. green onion, finely chopped

Directions

- In a pan of water, cook the potatoes till done completely and drain.
- Keep aside to cool completely.
- In a bowl, mix together the remaining ingredients except the green onion.
- Fold in the potatoes and green onion.
- Refrigerate for about 1 hour.

Amount per serving: 8

Timing Information:

Preparation	10 mins
Total Time	1 hr 40 mins

Nutritional Information:

Calories	173.5
Fat	3.5g
Cholesterol	2.5mg
Sodium	101.5mg
Carbohydrates	32.9g
Protein	3.7g

* Percent Daily Values are based on a 2,000 calorie diet.

Prawn Tapas Spanish Style

INGREDIENTS

- 2 lb raw king prawns, peeled and butterflied
- 3 tbsp parsley, chopped
- 1 tsp chili flakes
- 4 tbsp olive oil
- 4 -6 garlic cloves, thinly sliced
- 4 -6 tbsp dry sherry

Directions

- Set your oven to 400 degrees F before doing anything else.
- Carefully, slit the prawns lengthwise but don't go all the way through and remove the vein.
- In 6 small oven proof dishes, divide the prawns, garlic, chili flakes, sherry and olive oil.
- Cook in the oven for about 8-12 minutes.
- Serve with a sprinkle of the parsley alongside the crusty bread & lemon wedges.

Amount per serving: 6

Timing Information:

Preparation	5 mins
Total Time	13 mins

Nutritional Information:

Calories	285.0
Fat	11.6g
Cholesterol	228.0mg
Sodium	230.4mg
Carbohydrates	3.7g
Protein	30.7g

* Percent Daily Values are based on a 2,000 calorie diet.

Flame Broiled Chicken

INGREDIENTS

- 1 lb boneless skinless chicken breast, cut into 1/2 inch pieces
- 1 C. mayonnaise
- 1 medium red pepper, finely chopped
- 1 clove garlic
- 1 tsp red pepper flakes

Directions

- Soak 12 (8-inch) wooden skewers in water for about 30 minutes.
- Thread the chicken pieces onto presoaked skewers and in shallow baking dish.
- In a bowl, mix together the remaining ingredients and place over the skewers.
- Cot the chicken pieces with the marinade and refrigerate for about 30 minutes.
- Set the oven to broiler and arrange oven rack about 4-6-inches from heating element.
- Remove skewers from the refrigerator and discard the marinade.
- Arrange the skewers on the rack of a broiler pan.
- Cook under the broiler for about 10 minutes, flipping occasionally.

Amount per serving: 1

Timing Information:

Preparation	30 mins
Total Time	40 mins

Nutritional Information:

Calories	123.4
Fat	7.5g
Cholesterol	29.3mg
Sodium	183.6mg
Carbohydrates	5.4g
Protein	8.3g

* Percent Daily Values are based on a 2,000 calorie diet.

Traditional Tomato Tapas

(Tomates Rellenos)

INGREDIENTS

- 6 small tomatoes
- 3 eggs, hard-boiled, mashed
- 4 tbsp aioli
- salt, pepper
- 1 tbsp parsley, chopped
- olive oil

Directions

- Cut the tops off the tomatoes.
- Remove the core and seeds of the tomatoes with a spoon.
- In a bowl, mix together the parsley, eggs, aioli, salt and black pepper.
- Stuff the tomatoes with the parsley mixture and cover with the top slice.
- Drizzle with some olive oil and sprinkle with the black pepper.

Amount per serving: 6

Timing Information:

Preparation	30 mins
Total Time	30 mins

Nutritional Information:

Calories	53.3
Fat	2.6g
Cholesterol	105.7mg
Sodium	39.9mg
Carbohydrates	3.8g
Protein	3.9g

* Percent Daily Values are based on a 2,000 calorie diet.

Sevilla

INGREDIENTS

- 1 lb plum tomato, cored seeded and cut into small dice (ripe)
- 1/2 red onion, diced
- 1/4 C. capers, drained (tiny)
- 2 tbsp extra virgin olive oil
- 1/4 tsp black pepper, coarsely ground
- 2 tbsp flat leaf parsley, chopped

Directions

- In a bowl, mix together all the ingredients.
- Keep aside for about 1 hour before serving.

Amount per serving: 6

Timing Information:

Preparation	10 mins
Total Time	10 mins

Nutritional Information:

Calories	59.2
Fat	4.7g
Cholesterol	0.0mg
Sodium	174.8mg
Carbohydrates	4.3g
Protein	0.9g

* Percent Daily Values are based on a 2,000 calorie diet.

REAL SPANISH TAPAS

INGREDIENTS

- 3 tbsp olive oil
- 1 large onion, thinly sliced
- 3 medium potatoes, peeled and thinly sliced
- 2 garlic cloves, crushed
- 2 large red peppers, quartered, seeded and thinly sliced
- 6 large eggs, lightly beaten
- 1/2 tsp dried crushed red pepper flakes
- 1/4 C. flat leaf parsley, chopped

Directions

- Set your oven to degrees 400 F before doing anything else.
- In a large skillet, heat 2 tbsp of the oil on medium heat and cook the potatoes and onion for about 15 minutes, stirring occasionally.
- Add peppers and garlic and cook for about 5 minutes.
- Transfer the mixture into a bowl and keep aside for about 5 minutes.
- Stir in the eggs, parsley and chili flakes and keep aside for about 5 minutes.
- Place a 20cm square tin in the oven to heat for about 5 minutes.
- Remove the tin from the oven and coat with the oil.

- Place the egg mixture in the oven and cook in the oven for about 15-20 minutes.
- Remove from the oven and keep aside for about 5 minutes.
- Cut into desired sized squares and serve.

Amount per serving: 16

Timing Information:

Preparation	10 mins
Total Time	1 hr 10 mins

Nutritional Information:

Calories	90.9
Fat	4.5g
Cholesterol	79.3mg
Sodium	30.0mg
Carbohydrates	9.5g
Protein	3.5g

* Percent Daily Values are based on a 2,000 calorie diet.

Cilantro Shrimp Tapas

INGREDIENTS

- 1/4 C. extra virgin olive oil
- 3 canned jalapeno peppers, minced
- 3 garlic cloves, chopped
- 8 oz. fresh cooked shrimp, coarsely chopped
- 3 tbsp cilantro, chopped
- 1/2 tsp paprika
- salt
- 16 slices baguette

Directions

- In a large skillet, heat the oil and sauté the garlic and jalapeño for about 1 minute.
- Add the shrimp and cook for about 2 minutes.
- Stir in the cilantro, paprika and salt and cook till heated through.

Amount per serving: 4

Timing Information:

Preparation	10 mins
Total Time	15 mins

Nutritional Information:

Calories	935.4
Fat	19.3g
Cholesterol	119.5mg
Sodium	2126.8mg
Carbohydrates	147.0g
Protein	43.3g

* Percent Daily Values are based on a 2,000 calorie diet.

Honey Mustard Chicken Breast Girona Style Tapas

INGREDIENTS

- 3 chicken breasts, cut in to bite sized pieces
- 3 eggs
- flour, sufficient to coat the chicken pieces
- 5 tbsp olive oil
- salt & freshly ground black pepper

HONEY MUSTARD SAUCE:

- 1/2 C. honey
- 1 tbsp Dijon mustard
- 1 tsp soy sauce

Directions

- In a bowl, mix together the chicken and eggs.
- Add the flour and mix till well combined.
- In a large skillet, heat the oil and fry the chicken till golden from all the sides.
- Remove from the heat and season with the salt and black pepper.
- For sauce in a bowl, mix together all the ingredients.
- Pour the sauce over the chicken and serve.

Amount per serving: 8

Timing Information:

Preparation	20 mins
Total Time	40 mins

Nutritional Information:

Calories	261.0
Fat	15.3g
Cholesterol	104.5mg
Sodium	125.0mg
Carbohydrates	17.7g
Protein	13.9g

* Percent Daily Values are based on a 2,000 calorie diet.

Yummiest Potato Tapas

INGREDIENTS

- 2 large onions, chopped finely
- 5 tbsp olive oil
- 3 baking potatoes, like russets, peeled and cut into 1/4-inch cubes
- 1/4 tsp saffron thread
- 1/4 C. chicken broth
- 6 large eggs
- 1/2 C. thinly sliced scallion top
- salt & freshly ground black pepper

Directions

- In a large nonstick skillet, heat 2 tbsp of the oil on medium heat and sauté the onion for about 20 minutes.
- Remove from the heat and keep aside to cool completely.
- In a pan of salted boiling water, coo the potatoes for about 8 minutes.
- Drain well and keep aside to cool, then place into the bowl of the onion.
- In a small bowl, crumble the saffron threads.
- In a small pan heat the broth till hot.
- Pour the hot broth over the saffron and keep aside for about 5 minutes.

- In a large bowl, add the eggs, scallion greens, saffron mixture, salt and pepper and beat well.
- Fold in the onion and potato mixture.
- In skillet, heat remaining 3 tbsp of the oil on medium-high heat and add the egg mixture, spreading potatoes evenly.
- Reduce the heat to medium and cook the omelet for about 1 minute, stirring occasionally.
- Shift the skillet so that 1/4 of omelet is directly over center of burner and cook for about 1 minute.
- Shift the skillet 3 more times, cooking remaining fourths in the same way.
- Center the skillet and cook omelet over low heat for about 4 minutes more.
- Carefully, invert the omelet into the skillet. and cook for about 4 minutes.

Amount per serving: 8

Timing Information:

| Preparation | 1 hr |
| Total Time | 1 hr |

Nutritional Information:

Calories	190.8
Fat	12.1g
Cholesterol	139.5mg
Sodium	81.3mg
Carbohydrates	14.5g
Protein	6.3g

* Percent Daily Values are based on a 2,000 calorie diet.

Fennel and Coriander Olives

INGREDIENTS

- 1 lb green olives
- 6 garlic cloves, sliced
- 1 tbsp crushed coriander seed
- 1 tbsp crushed fennel seed
- 6 fresh thyme sprigs
- 4 rosemary sprigs
- 1 orange, zest of
- 1 orange, juice of
- olive oil

Directions

- In a bowl, add all the ingredients except the olive oil and transfer into a jar.
- Add enough oil that covers the olives.
- Cover the jar and shake well.
- Keep in room temperature for about 6 days.

Amount per serving: 8

Timing Information:

Preparation	5 mins
Total Time	10 mins

Nutritional Information:

Calories	94.8
Fat	8.9g
Cholesterol	0.0mg
Sodium	884.3mg
Carbohydrates	4.7g
Protein	0.9g

* Percent Daily Values are based on a 2,000 calorie diet.

Orange Blossom Bread Sticks

INGREDIENTS

- 1 (8 oz.) packets breadsticks
- 3 oz. orange blossom honey
- 4 oz. serrano ham, in thin slices

Directions

- Coat the tips of bread sticks in the honey and then drain.
- Wrap the ham slices around the bread sticks.

Amount per serving: 8

Timing Information:

Preparation	5 mins
Total Time	5 mins

Nutritional Information:

Calories	261.0
Fat	15.3g
Cholesterol	104.5mg
Sodium	125.0mg
Carbohydrates	17.7g
Protein	13.9g

* Percent Daily Values are based on a 2,000 calorie diet.

Thanks for Reading! Now Let's Try some Sushi and Dump Dinners....

http://bit.ly/2443TFg

To grab this **box set** simply follow the link mentioned above, or tap the book cover.

This will take you to a page where you can simply enter your email address and a PDF version of the **box set** will be emailed to you.

I hope you are ready for some serious cooking!

http://bit.ly/2443TFg

You will also receive updates about all my new books when they are free.

Also don't forget to like and subscribe on the social networks. I love meeting my readers. Links to all my profiles are below so please click and connect :)

Facebook

Twitter

Come On...
Let's Be Friends :)

I adore my readers and love connecting with them socially. Please follow the links below so we can connect on Facebook, Twitter, and Google+.

Facebook

Twitter

I also have a blog that I regularly update for my readers so check it out below.

My Blog

Can I Ask A Favour?

If you found this book interesting, or have otherwise found any benefit in it. Then may I ask that you post a review of it on Amazon? Nothing excites me more than new reviews, especially reviews which suggest new topics for writing. I do read all reviews and I always factor feedback into my newer works.

So if you are willing to take ten minutes to write what you sincerely thought about this book then please visit our Amazon page and post your opinions.

Again thank you!

INTERESTED IN OTHER EASY COOKBOOKS?

Everything is easy! Check out my Amazon Author page for more great cookbooks:

For a complete listing of all my books please see my author page.

Made in the USA
Lexington, KY
18 December 2016